Famous & Fun Duets

6 Duets for One Piano, Four Hands

Carol Matz

Famous & Fun Duets, Book 2, contains carefully selected familiar songs and timeless masterworks of the great composers. The duets are arranged in equal parts for early elementary to elementary pianists, and are written for one piano, four hands. For easier reading, each part is written using both treble and bass clefs, with directions for the *primo* to play up an octave and the *secondo* down an octave. Additionally, the melody often shifts between *primo* and *secondo,* creating interesting parts for both players. No eighth notes or dotted-quarter rhythms are used. Students are sure to enjoy their experience with these fun duets!

Alfred

Alfred Music Publishing Co., Inc.
P.O. Box 10003
Van Nuys, CA 91410-0003
alfred.com

ISBN-10: 0-7390-7650-7
ISBN-13: 978-0-7390-7650-7

Can-Can

(from the operetta *Orpheus in the Underworld*)

Secondo

Jacques Offenbach
Arranged by Carol Matz

Quickly
Play both hands one octave lower

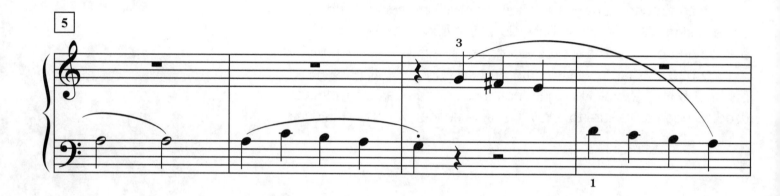

Can-Can

(from the operetta *Orpheus in the Underworld*)

Primo

Jacques Offenbach
Arranged by Carol Matz

Quickly
Play both hands one octave higher

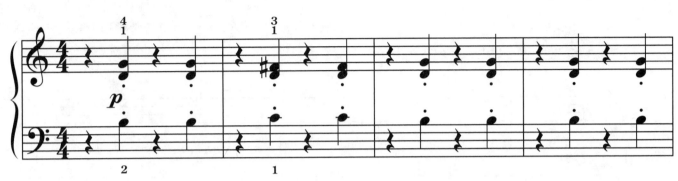

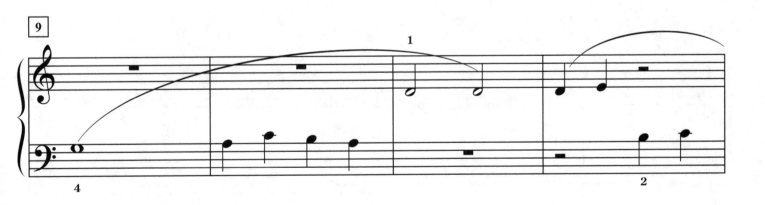

The Ants Go Marching

Secondo

Traditional
Arranged by Carol Matz

Quickly
Play both hands one octave lower

The ants go march-ing one by one, hur-

rah!   Hur - rah!   The

ants go march - ing one by one, hur -

rah!   Hur - rah!

The Ants Go Marching

Primo

Traditional
Arranged by Carol Matz

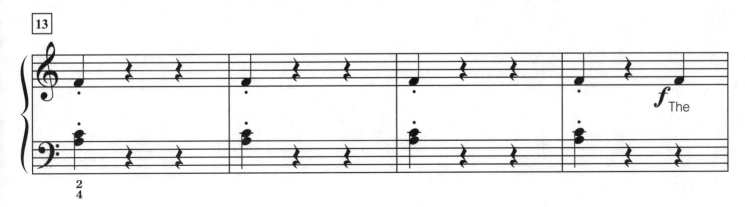

Secondo

8va

Primo

Barcarolle

(from the opera *The Tales of Hoffmann*)

Secondo

Jacques Offenbach
Arranged by Carol Matz

Moderately

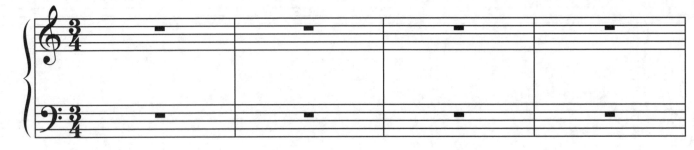

Play both hands one octave lower

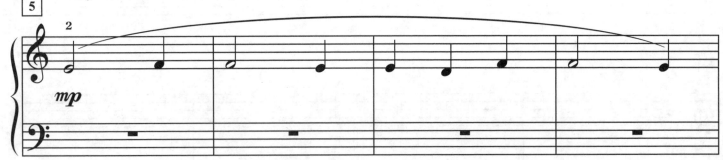

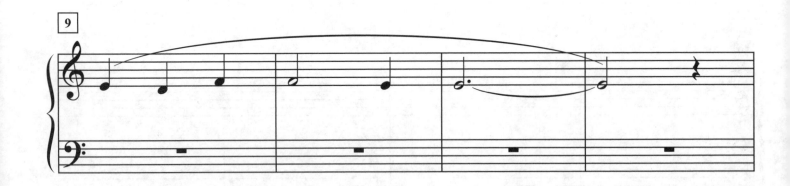

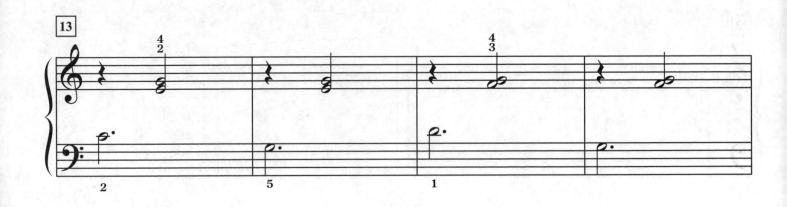

Barcarolle

(from the opera *The Tales of Hoffmann*)

Primo

Jacques Offenbach
Arranged by Carol Matz

Moderately
Play both hands one octave higher

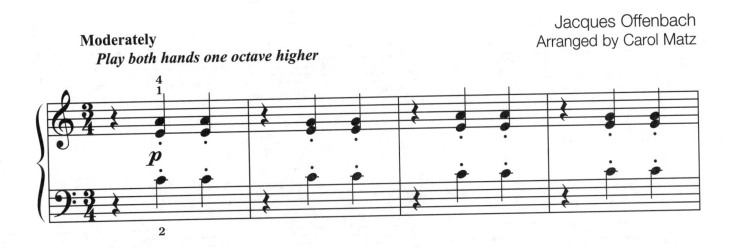

Secondo

Primo

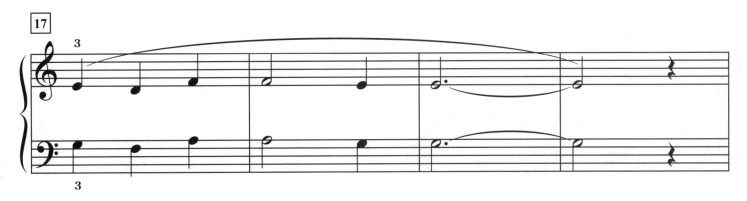

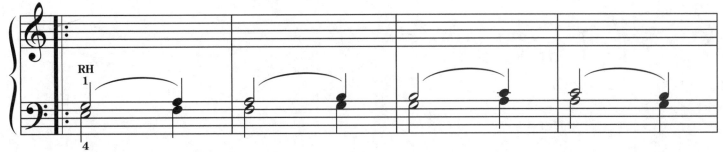

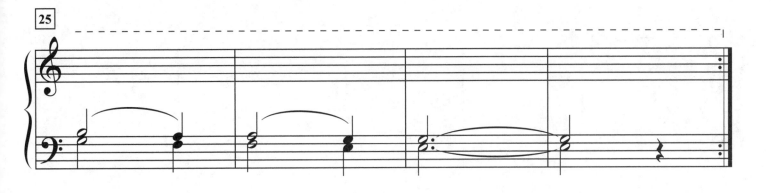

Secondo

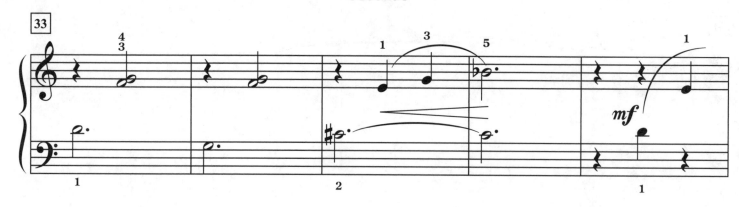

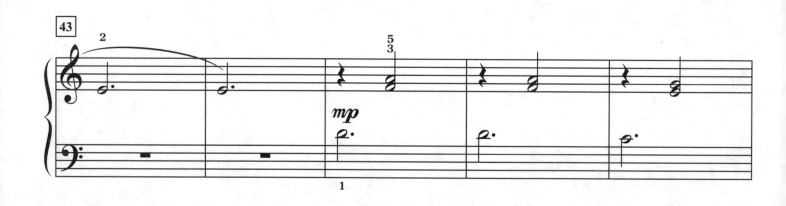

Primo

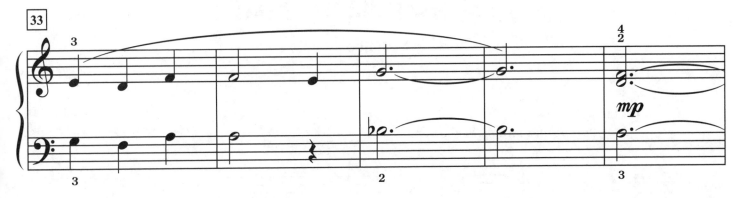

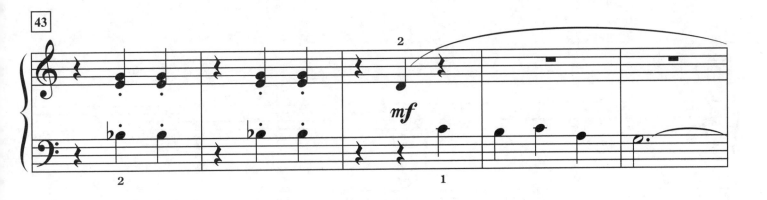

Scarborough Fair

Secondo

Traditional
Arranged by Carol Matz

Moderately slow
Play both hands one octave lower

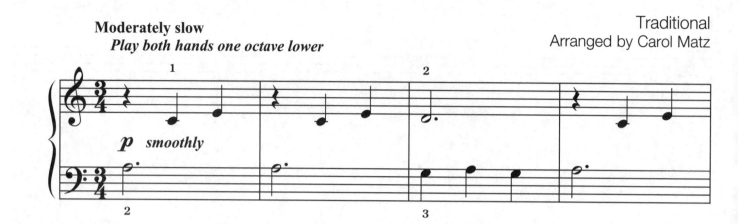

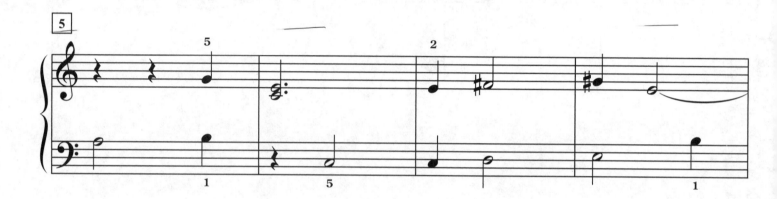

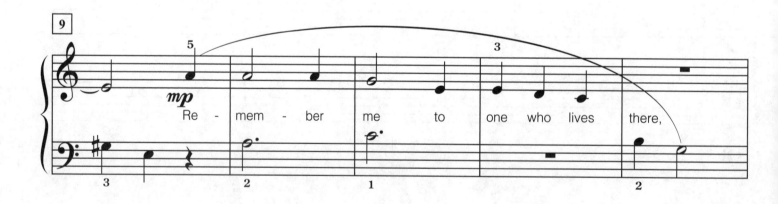

Scarborough Fair

Primo

Traditional
Arranged by Carol Matz

Moderately slow
Play both hands one octave higher

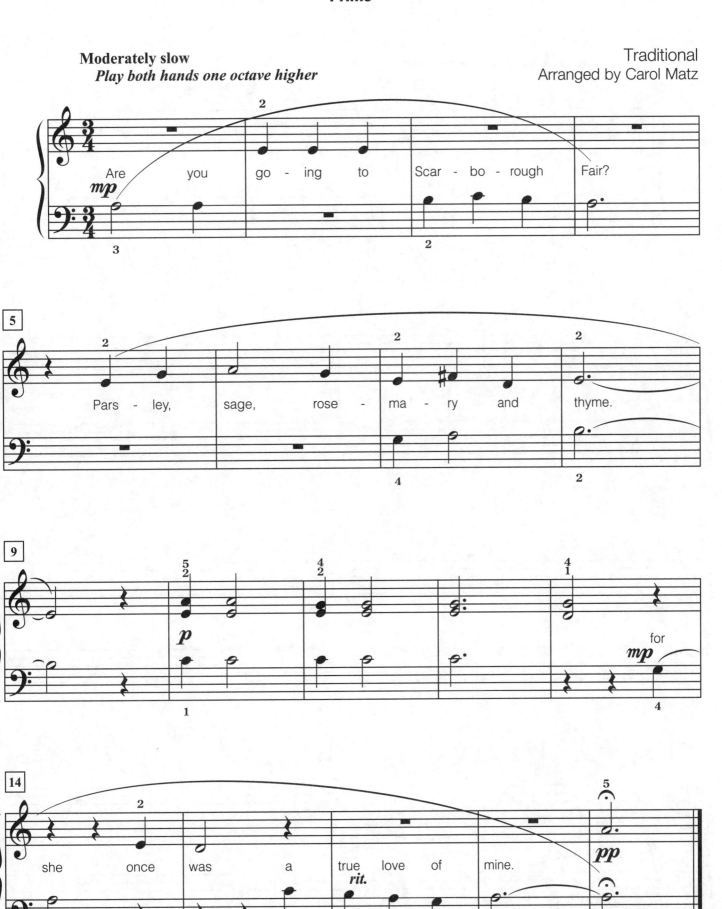

Maple Leaf Rag

Secondo

Scott Joplin
Arranged by Carol Matz

Moderately fast
Play both hands one octave lower

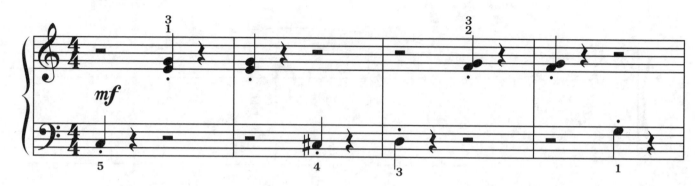

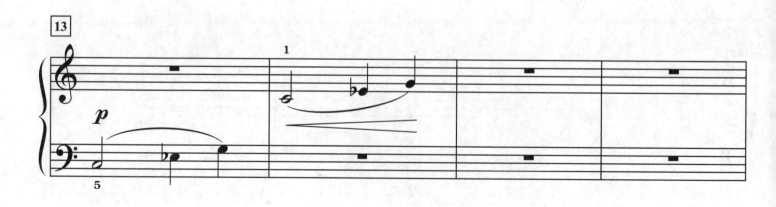

Maple Leaf Rag

Primo

Scott Joplin
Arranged by Carol Matz

Secondo

Primo

Theme from Symphony No. 5

(First Movement)

Secondo

Ludwig van Beethoven
Arranged by Carol Matz

Fast
Play both hands one octave lower

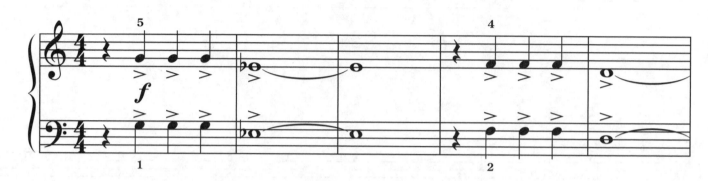

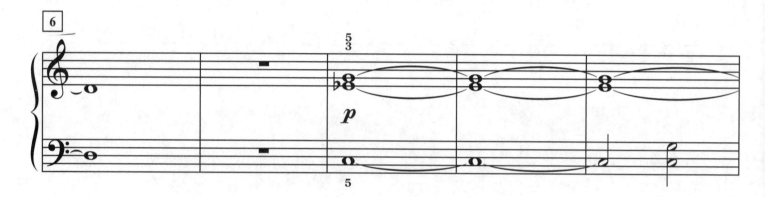

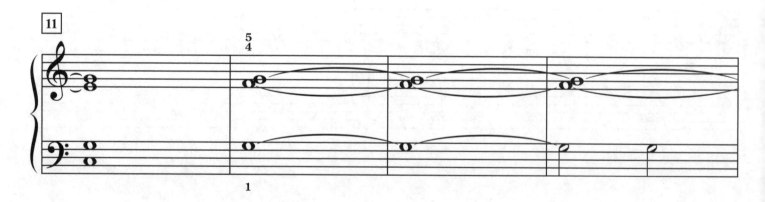

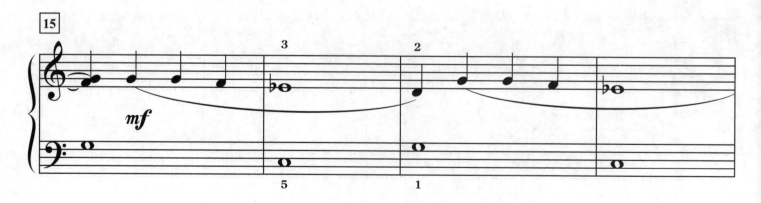

Theme from Symphony No. 5

(First Movement)

Primo

Ludwig van Beethovan
Arranged by Carol Matz

Fast
Play both hands one octave higher

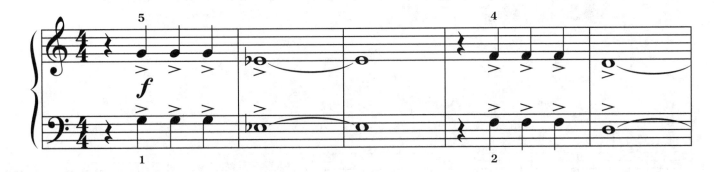

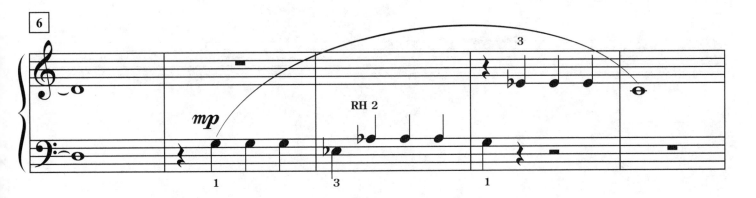

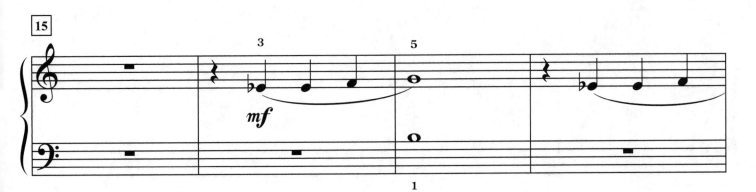

Secondo

Primo

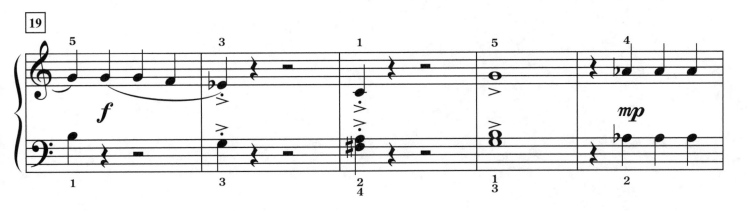

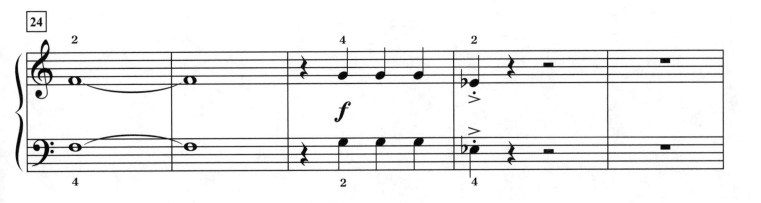

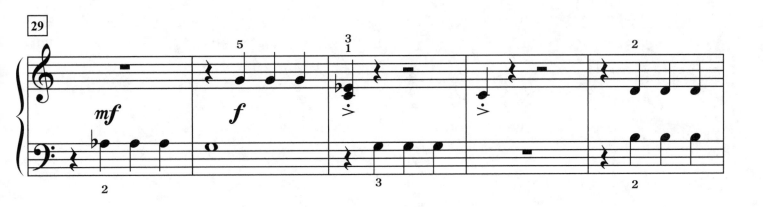

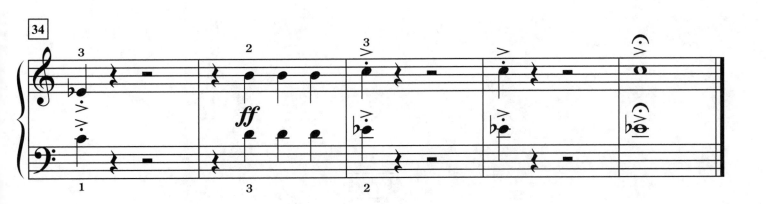